What If They Could Fly?

Dona Herweck Rice

Publishing Credits
Rachelle Cracchiolo, M.S.Ed., *Publisher*
Conni Medina, M.A.Ed., *Managing Editor*
Nika Fabienke, Ed.D., *Content Director*
Véronique Bos, *Creative Director*
Shaun N. Bernadou, *Art Director*
Seth Rogers, *Editor*
John Leach, *Assistant Editor*
Courtney Roberson, *Senior Graphic Designer*

Image Credits: All images from iStock and/or Shutterstock.

Library of Congress Cataloging-in-Publication Data
Names: Rice, Dona, author.
Title: What if they could fly? / Dona Herweck Rice.
Description: Huntington Beach, CA : Teacher Created Materials, [2019] | Identifiers: LCCN 2018029752 (print) | LCCN 2018033701 (ebook) | ISBN 9781493899470 | ISBN 9781493898732
Subjects: LCSH: Readers (Primary)
Classification: LCC PE1119 (ebook) | LCC PE1119 .R469 2019 (print) | DDC 428.6/2--dc23
LC record available at https://lccn.loc.gov/2018029752

Teacher Created Materials
5301 Oceanus Drive
Huntington Beach, CA 92649-1030
www.tcmpub.com
ISBN 978-1-4938-9873-2
© 2019 Teacher Created Materials, Inc.
Printed in China
Nordica.082018.CA21800936

What if a  could  ?

dog

fly

What if a
cat

could  ?
fly

What if a

rat

could  ?

fly

What if a could  ?

horse

fly

What if a

cow

could  ?

fly

What if a
pig

could ✈ ?
fly

What if a

snake

could ✈ ?

fly

What if a

turtle

could  ?

fly

What if a

baby

could  ?

fly

What if a

grandma

could  ?

fly

High-Frequency Words

New Words

could if

what

Review Word

a